Medieval Times

S T E V E   B U X T O N

Acknowledgements

The publishers would like to thank the following for permission to reproduce copyright illustrations:

British Library – page 11 (folio 193 from additional ms 42130), page 39 (Cott Augustus I folio 83), page 30 (ms 18 E I folio 172), page 34 (ms 2A XXII folio 220); Cambridge University Library – page 28; Master and Fellows of Corpus Christi College, Cambridge – page 38; DFSD – pages 35 and 37; C M Dixon – page 28; Sonia Halliday Photography – pages 36, 38 and 44; Master and Fellows of Trinity College, Cambridge – page 11.

British Library Cataloguing in Publication Data
Buxton, Steven
  Medieval Times.- (Action history; Bk 2).
  1. History
  I. Title   II. Series
  942

  ISBN 0–340–51897–9

First published 1991
Impression number   10   9   8   7
Year   1998   1997

Illustrations by Joseph McEwan

Typeset by Taurus Graphics, Abingdon, Oxon
Printed for Hodder & Stoughton Educational, a division of Hodder Headline Plc, 338 Euston Road, London NW1 3BH by Colorcraft Ltd, Hong Kong

Contents

The Medieval Village

> **medieval,** village, **villein,** cottage, graze,
> common, religious

This book tells you about life long ago. About
700 years ago. This is known as the medieval part
of our history.

In those days life was very different. Most
people lived in villages. They were farmers. A
village might have looked like this.

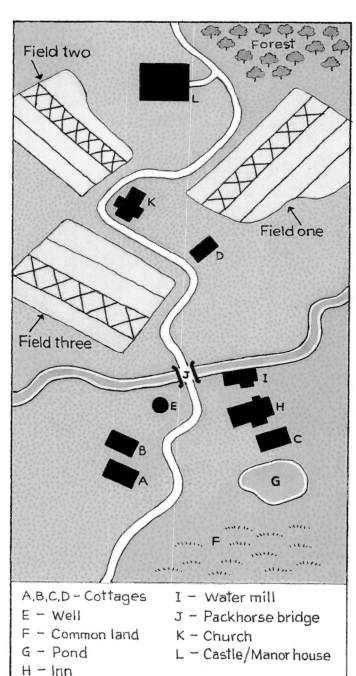

A,B,C,D – Cottages	I – Water mill
E – Well	J – Packhorse bridge
F – Common land	K – Church
G – Pond	L – Castle/Manor house
H – Inn	

John,
a *villein*

Hello. My name is John. I live in a small cottage in the village. I spend most of my time farming. It is very hard work. There are about twenty people in the village like me. We are the villeins.
We grow crops for food. We farm strips of land in the fields. Look at the map of the village. You can see the strips which I farm. They are marked like this. XXXX

My name is Mary. I am John's wife. So John thinks he works hard eh! He should try being a woman.
I look after the children in our family. I have to cook, take care of our *cottage* and fetch water from the well. Sometimes I do some spinning to make clothes. And often I take the children to the fields. Just like John we work many hard hours on the land.

I am George, the cowherd. Most of the villagers have a cow or pig. I look after their animals during the day.
The animals all *graze* on the *common*. I have to make sure they do not get into the fields and damage the crops. The fields do not have any fences you see.

I am Cedric, the miller. I have an important job. I grind the corn to make flour for bread. I keep some of the corn myself as payment for my work.

I am Father Cross, the parish priest. I look after the church and tell people about God and the bible. The villagers are very *religious*. They have to share their food with me.

I am Lord Fitzherbert, the Lord of the manor. I am in charge of the village. I have many servants. The villeins must work on my land for two or three days each week and obey my orders.

WORKFILE

1 Look at the map of the village on page 4. Think about where each of the people in the village might have lived.

Copy and complete this table. Match up the people and their homes from the picture on page 1. The first line has already been filled in.

Person	Where they lived
John	Cottage A
Mary	
Cowherd	
Miller	
Priest	
Lord	

2 Answer these questions. Write a sentence for each one.
  a How many strips did John farm?
  b What was made in the water mill?
  c Where did people get their water from?
  d Where might people get their firewood?

3 Here is a list of things you can find in a modern village. Write down those which you might also find in a medieval village:

pub, farm houses, school, post office, bus stop, church, cottages, stream, roads, trees, cows, old people's home, garage, canal, hedges, cars, mill, common, well.

4 Copy the sentences below and fill in the missing words from those given.

● also, each, cowherd, animals, They.

Many villeins lived in the village. _____ villein farmed some strips of land. _____ grew food to eat. Many villeins _____ kept a cow or a pig. The _____ grazed together on the common. The _____ looked after them.

● food, shared, person, finest, work.

The lord was the most important _____ . He lived in the manor house. He did not _____ in the fields. The villeins grew _____ for him. Often the church was the _____ building in the village. The villeins _____ their food with the priest.

Home, Sweet Home

Inside John and Mary's cottage

---

hob, trestle

Inside John's cottage there is one room. John and his family share their home with their animals.

The fire is in the middle of the room. It is made on a large iron plate, or hob. Smoke swirls around the room as there is no chimney. It escapes through the door, small window holes or cracks in the wall. The fire is used for cooking and for warmth.

There are not many windows. They are just small holes in the wall. There is no glass. It is dark inside the cottage.

The floor is made of earth, trodden down or beaten hard. It is very muddy in wet weather. Sometimes it is covered with straw.

There is not much furniture. A few stools, a trestle table and a chest to store clothes in. Water comes from the well or from the river. It has to be carried in a wooden bucket. Outside there is a hole dug in the ground. This is used as a toilet.

WORKFILE

1 Draw a table like the one below, listing these items down the left-hand side:

windows, cooking, number of rooms, walls, heating, floor, water supply, washing, toilets.

Fill in the table to show the differences between your home and a villein's home.

	Villein's home	**My home**
windows	holes	glass
cooking	on fire	on cooker
Number of rooms		

2 Draw a picture to show what it might have been like in John's cottage. Label your picture. Use these labels:

earth floor   fire   hole in roof   small window   table   chest   smoke.

2 Farming

sowing, ploughing, furrow, oxen

These pictures were drawn in medieval times. They show some of the jobs which the villeins did in the fields.

Source A

This picture shows villeins ploughing the land.

Source B

This man is sowing seeds. You can see the furrows left in the soil by the plough.

Source C

See if you can work out what these two people are doing. (Do the others in your group agree?)

WORKFILE

1 Study source A carefully and answer these questions.

   a What does the plough do to the soil?

b What do you think the plough is made of?

c How many oxen are pulling the plough?

d What are the two people doing?

2 Look at the man in source B. Write a few lines to describe what he is doing. Use some of these words to help you:

- throw, trudge, sweat, scoop.
- ground, apron, mud, hand, furrows.

3 Write a sentence or two to say what you think each of the two people in source C is doing.

The Villein Game

John the villein had a hard life. Most of his time was spent growing food to eat.

Play this game with the help of your teacher, and find out more about the life of a villein.

Aim

You hope to grow fifty baskets of corn this year. You will use it for food for your family. Fifty baskets will be plenty. But if you grow less than ten baskets you will starve.

Get Ready

Make up a group of four to six players. Number six pieces of paper (1–6) and put them face down on your table (or use a die).

Draw a corn record table like the one shown below. Fill it in at the end of each round. (You start with fifty baskets, remember.)

What to Do

There are six rounds in the game. Each player picks up one piece of paper at the start of each round.

Round 1: Land given out

Look at your number. Look up your number on the game chart. What has happened to you? Tell the others in your group. Write it down on your corn record table, and fill in your score.

Round 2: Preparing the land

Put your number papers back in the middle.

Pick a new number. What has happened to you this time? Tell the others and fill in your corn record.

Carry on with the other rounds.

At the End

Look at your corn record. Work out how many baskets you have left to eat.

WORKFILE

1 Have you got enough to eat?
2 What happens if you finish with less than ten baskets?
3 What was the worst thing that happened to you in the game?
4 What was the best thing?
5 Who grew the most food in your group? How much did they grow?

Round	What happened	Baskets of corn		Total
		gained	**lost**	**(out of 50)**
1	(e.g. Poor strip – (stony ground)	—	2	48
2				

Game Chart

All players: Target: 50 baskets   Minimum to survive: 10 baskets

	1	2	3	4	5	6
Land given out Round 1	Bad strip. Near river. Very marshy Lose 30 baskets	Poor strip. Long walk from the village Lose 10 baskets	Poor strip. Stony ground Lose 2 baskets	Very good strip. Rich, fertile soil Gain 4 baskets	Quite good strip. In middle of field. Gain 1 basket	Good strip. Well drained. Close to village. Gain 3 baskets
Preparing the land Round 2	Weak horses. Don't plough very well Lose 1 basket	Good ploughman. Straight lines Gain 2 baskets	Wooden plough breaks. Time lost on repairs. Lose 1 basket	Good ploughman. Very quick Gain 2 baskets	Rainy day. Soil sticks to plough Lose 1 basket	Strong oxen. Pull plough quickly Gain 3 baskets
Sowing the seed Round 3	Windy day. Seeds blow away Lose 5 baskets	Birds eat seeds as you sow Lose 10 baskets	You get arm ache and don't throw well Lose 20 baskets	You drop the seeds and waste a lot Lose 2 baskets	Good sowing Gain 5 baskets	Good sowing Gain 5 baskets
Growing the crops Round 4	Perfect summer weather Gain 15 baskets	Quite good summer Gain 5 baskets	Thunderstorm destroys your crops Lose 10 baskets	Dry summer. Wheat withers away Lose 3 baskets	Good summer Gain 10 baskets	Wet summer. Wheat can not ripen Lose 6 baskets
Harvest Round 5	Blunt scythe. Damages crop Lose 5 baskets	Good harvest. With extra help from your family Gain 8 baskets	Some of your crop is trampled by the children Lose 5 baskets	Good harvest in fine weather Gain 10 baskets	You drink too much ale when harvesting Lose 15 baskets	Good harvest. With extra help from your family Gain 8 baskets
Storing Round 6	Mice in the barn eat much of your crop Lose 20 baskets	Damp barn. Some of your crop goes rotten Lose 15 baskets	Good barn. Sound and dry Gain 2 baskets	Barn catches fire Lose all your crop	Good barn. Sound and dry Gain 2 baskets	Mice in the barn eat much of your crop Lose 20 baskets

3 A Ploughman's Poem

crede, sorrowful, **source, evidence**

	line
And as I went on my way,	1
I saw a poor man over the plough bending.	2
His hood was full of holes	3
And his hair sticking out,	4
His shoes were patched.	5
His toes peeped out as he the ground trod.	6
His wife walked by him	7
In a skirt cut full high.	8
Wrapped in a sheet to keep her from the weather.	9
Bare foot on the bare ice	10
so that the blood flowed.	11
And at the field's end lay a little bowl,	12
And in there lay a little child wrapped in rags	13
And two more of two years old upon another side.	14
And all of them sang a song	15
That was *sorrowful* to hear.	16
They all cried a cry,	17
A sorrowful note.	18
And the poor man sighed sore and said	19
'Children be still.'	20

The poem on the left is called 'The crede of Piers the Ploughman'. It was written by William Langland about 600 years ago.

WORKFILE

1 Choose the best ending for these sentences and copy them down.

    a The man was _____.
     (*threshing, sowing, ploughing*)

b There were holes in his hood and

_____ .

(*shoes, coat, trousers*)

c His wife was _____ .

(*walking by his side, spinning and weaving, looking after the children*)

d She had no shoes and her feet were bleeding because she cut them on the

_____ .

(*stones, ice, plough*)

e The children sang a _____ song.

(*happy, loud, sad*)

f The man told the children to be quiet with a

_____ .

(*roar, sigh, wave of his arm*)

2 This is a sad poem. Read it again. Pick out all the words which make it sound sad. Make up a table like this one and complete it.

line number	words
2 3	poor man full of holes

3 Write a poem in your own words to tell the ploughman's tale.

4 The children in Willian Langland's poem went with their parents to work in the fields. What do children do these days while their parents work? Make a list of at least four things. Do the others in your group agree with you?

5 Look at the pictures on page 9 (farming).

Compare them with what the poem tells you. Do these sources agree or disagree?

(What do the others in your group think?)

Copy the table below. What do the pictures show about children in the fields? Fill in box X. What does the poem show (maybe nothing). Fill in box Y.

Do your sentences agree or disagree? Complete the table.

 History Jury

Which one tells the truth?
You are acting like the jury in a court. They have to decide which evidence to believe.

Think about the sources. Which evidence do you believe? Which tells the truth? Might they all be true? (Do the others in your group agree with you?)

Write two or three sentences to say which one you believe the most.

	(pictures)	(poem)	agree/ disagree
Women in fields	There are no women.	The poor man's wife is with him in the field	disagree
Children in fields	X	Y	
Clothes			
Footwear			
The mood of the villeins			

4

Mary's Life

Darn – mend a hole in clothes

---

spinning, thread, earn, **darn**, rushes,
paving, quotation

Besides working in the fields women worked
hard in the home. They sometimes earned a little
extra money by spinning. *(pay for food/rent)*

The woman on the left of the picture is
spinning. She is making woollen thread on a
spinning machine. After a while her arms begin
to ache. Later the woollen thread will be made
into clothes.

This picture was drawn in medieval times. *PRIMARY SOURCE*
Here is another source. It was written by Willian
Langland. *SECONDARY SOURCE*

Source A

'They earn by spinning. They spend on rent, milk
or porridge to stop the crying of the children.
They themselves suffer much hunger. They wake
at midnight to rock the cradle, darn clothes and
wash them, and put rushes on the paving.'

WORKFILE

1 Make a drawing of a medieval
woman spinning. *(H/W)*

2 Look at the five picture frames at
the bottom of this page. They show
some scenes as described by Langland in Source
A.

Copy each of the frames. *(Cut + paste)*

3 Read Source A again. Choose some short
quotations to go with your drawings. Write a
quotation under each of your drawings. The first
one is done for you.

Rock the cradle

The Good Fairy Strikes Again

2 Ten kilos of oats

1 One year's supply of rushes for the floor

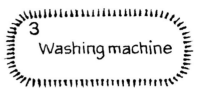
3 Washing machine

10 One year's free rent

4 A cow

9 100 litres of milk

5 A nanny for the children

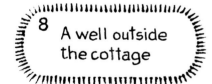
8 A well outside the cottage

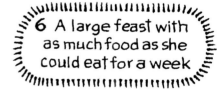
6 A large feast with as much food as she could eat for a week

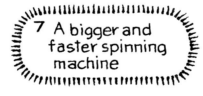
7 A bigger and faster spinning machine

WORKFILE

1 You are the good fairy. You can grant Mary three wishes. She can choose three from the ten wishes above.

2 Write three sentences to say why you think she will choose these. (Have the others in your group chosen the same three?)

Points to bear in mind:
- No electricity.
- No fridges.
- No piped water.
- Everybody in the village could graze animals on the common.
- Servants need feeding.

5 Lord and Villein

duties, **tithes,** permission

I do not own any land. The lord lets me have strips of land to farm. On these strips we grow food for the family. The lord owns the cottage we live in as well.

Of course we have to pay our lord. We do not have much money so usually we pay him in other ways. Sometimes we give him food, eggs maybe. Sometimes we do *duties*. We might work on his land for one day a week.

We have to pay *tithes* to the Church too. This means we give them one tenth of everything we make or grow.

This system has its good points. At least our family has enough land to feed itself. We can keep our animals on the common. If there is trouble the lord protects us with his armed men. The lord and priest keep law and order in the village.

But I do not really like things the way they are. We have to put the lord's work first, even if our own strips need working on. We are not allowed to leave the manor and live somewhere else.

John's land   Fitzherbert's land

WORKFILE

1 Copy the flow chart below. Write a sentence or two to fill in the two empty boxes. In one box write in what duties the villein was expected to do for the lord. In the other box write in the duties which the villein was expected to do for the Church.

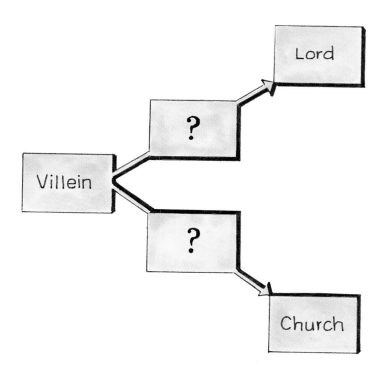

2 Copy the following paragraph and fill in the missing words. Choose from these words:

village, produce, had, They, did, tithe.

Villeins did not own any land. _____ rented strips from the lord. They _____ duties to pay the rent. They _____ to work on the lord's land. They had to give one tenth of all their _____ to the Church. This was called a _____ . They could not move away from the _____ without the lord's permission.

3 Now you know how John's village was organised. Think about who would have been most happy with things as they were. The villeins? The lord? The Church?

Copy this table and fill it in. Show who you think would have liked or disliked the things in the table. (See if the others in your group agree with you.)

Like = L
Dislike = D
Don't know = DK

The first one is done for you. (Do the others in your group agree with you?)

	Lord	Priest	Villein
Villeins paid tithes to the Church	DK	L	D
Lord kept order in the village			
Villeins did duties on the lord's land (and sometimes Church land).			
Villeins needed permission to leave the village.			
Villeins could grow food for themselves.			
The lord owned the villein's cottage.			
Villeins had to do the lord's work first.			

The Feudal System

baron, loyalty, king

You know that John had to do duties for his lord of the manor. In medieval England the lord also had to be loyal to more important lords called barons. Lords had to pay money and do duties for the barons. (For example, they had to provide soldiers for a baron's army.)

In turn, even the barons had to swear loyalty and pay money to the most important lord of all, the king. The king could call upon the barons, lords and their soldiers to fight for him if they were needed.

All this was called the 'Feudal System'.

WORKFILE

1 Copy this diagram of the 'Feudal System'. Write a sentence where there is a question mark. Say what duties the person below had to do for the person above.

THE KING

_____ ?

BARONS

_____ ?

LORDS OF THE MANOR

_____ ?

VILLEINS

2 Draw a picture beside your diagram to show how the feudal system worked.

6 The Black Death

disease, epidemic, plague, symptom,
knowledge, prevent, victim

During the year 1347 a terrible disease appeared
in Europe. It caused an epidemic. It spread
quickly from village to village, but no one knew
how. People who caught the disease nearly
always died within a few days.

Some towns and villages got off lightly. In
other villages everyone died. The disease was
called a plague. Some people called it the 'Black
Death'. It spread through most of Britain in 1348
and 1349. Writers at the time described the
coming of the Black Death.

Source A

'We see death coming like a black smoke,
terrible wherever it may come . . . a head
that gives pain and causes a loud cry . . . a
burden carried under the arms, a painful
angry white lump that spares no one.'

Then new symptoms showed:

Source B

'Black spots making their appearance on the
arm or thigh, a sign of approaching death.'

Stopping the Disease

No one understood what caused the Black Death.
There were lots of ideas but they did little good.
In those days there were few doctors and they
had little knowledge.

Modern day doctors can prevent the Black
Death with injections. We know what causes the
disease and how it spreads. But in medieval
times there was no escape.

WORKFILE

1 Draw a picture of a village badly
hit by the plague. Show victims of
the Black Death being buried.

Look at the pictures on the next
page to help you and remember . . .

- Many people would have died.
- The priest might have died.
- Few people would be left.
- They might have to be buried in a large grave
  or burial pit.

2 Use Sources A and B to find out four
symptoms of the Black Death. Write in your own
words what these symptoms were.

3 Look at Source C. Who do the three figures on the right represent?

Source C
Some medieval pictures try to remind people of the closeness of death

4 Look at Source D. Write a sentence or two to answer these questions:

   a Why are some people carrying coffins on their own?

   b Who do you think are burying the dead?

Source D   Victims of the Black Death being buried

The 'Vanishing Villeins' Game

The Black Death had a serious effect on many manors. Each person in your group is going to play the part of the lord of the manor. You each have a different manor. Although many lords died, you all survived the Black Death but many of the villeins from your manor died. What will happen to your manor?

Getting Ready

These pages will help you to get ready for the game. You will need to find paper and pens and you may need to copy the score card, if your teacher has not already made a copy for you.

Before the Black Death Arrives

All the manors have six villeins. This is enough to grow food for the lord. So all the lords are happy. But not for long.

This villein belongs to Lord _____.

Each player, or lord of the manor, should draw six villeins like this one, on six pieces of paper.

Give yourself a name, and write it on each piece of paper. Number them 1 to 6.

Aim

The aim of this game is to keep as many villeins as you can, so that the manor continues to produce enough food. Bear in mind:

● Once the Black Death comes, some villeins may die.
● If your manor no longer has enough villeins to work on it, you may have to pay workers to come from other manors to work on yours.
● This may be expensive — after all, your villeins worked for free.
● Your own villeins may be offered money to go and work for another lord.

There might not be enough villeins to go round. Which lord will end up with enough villeins? which lord will lose out?

Copy out this score card, to help you to keep a record of your progress.

Stage 1
Number of villeins _____ × 10 points = _____
                                                    +
Stage 2
Number of villeins _____ × 10 points = _____
                                                    +
Number of paid _____ × 5 points = _____
workers
                    Total points score = _____

Checklist

Before you begin to play, divide into groups of 3–6 players. Make sure that each player has:

- A name (you are Lord _____)
- 6 'villeins', numbered
- A score card.

Each group will also need:

- 6 pieces of paper numbered 1–6 (fold them up and put them in the middle)
- A large piece of paper labelled 'Burial Pit'. Place this in the middle.

I could pay money (wages) to villeins from other manors. They would leave their own manors and come and work on mine

How to Play

Scoring

You get points for each villein who works for you. You all start off with the same number of villeins (6). Villeins are worth 10 points. Paid workers are worth only 5 points.

Fill in line 1 of your score card. (You should all have scored 60 points so far.)

Stage 1: The Black Death Arrives

The dreaded Black Death hits your village. Many villeins die. Some villagers are hit worse than others.

Each player picks up one piece of numbered paper from the pile in the middle. This tells you how many of your villeins have died. Bury your dead villeins in the burial pit. Take them from the six you have drawn.

- Which lord was worst hit in your group? How many of his or her villeins died?
- What might happen to much of the land on this manor?

Paying the Villeins

After the Black Death many lords did not have enough villeins to farm their land on the manor. How could they get more villeins?

Stage 2: After the Black Death

You are going to pay money to try to get more villeins if you need them. Villeins from other manors will be attracted by the highest wages. Some lords will lose out.

- Try to end up with six villeins on your manor again.
- Try to keep your own villeins. You won't have to pay them. They will be worth more points.

Place the numbered papers back in the middle. Each player picks up a new number.

Your number tells you how much you can pay in wages to your villeins.

Look up your number on the game chart (see below). Read it out, then do what the chart tells you.

Highest number goes first. Lowest number goes last.

Some lords might end up with no villeins.

Scoring

Now fill in Stage 2 on your score card.

If you kept some of your own villeins they are worth 10 points.

Villeins from other manors have to be paid. They are only worth 5 points.

Add up your points total. The winner is the lord with the biggest total.

Game Chart

6	You can pay wages of 6 pence to every villein who works for you. The highest wages in the county. You get the first choice. Take as many villeins as you need from any of the other lords. No one can now take any of your villeins.
5	You pay wages of 5 pence to any villein who work for you. Take as many villeins as you need from lords with lower numbers than you. Too bad if they do not have enough. No one can now take any of your villeins.
4	As for number 5 but you pay wages of 4 pence.
3	As above but you pay wages of 3 pence. Too bad if there are not enough villeins left.
2	As above but you pay only 2 pence wages.
1	Hard luck. You pay only 1 pence wages so the villeins do not want to work for you. Have you got enough villeins?

WORKFILE

1 Which lord in your group was worst off after the Black Death? What might have happened to their manor?

2 Copy this table and tick one column to say if each statement was true or false.

The effects of the Black Death	True	False
There were not enough villeins to work all the land in England.		
All the lords were better off.		
The feudal system did not change.		
All villeins who survived the Black Death were better off.		
Many villeins earned money for the first time.		
No villeins left the manor they belonged to.		

Some effects of the Black Death

7 The Peasants' Revolt

tax, peasant, revolt, rebel, riot, archbishop, traitor

We have seen that the feudal system began to change after the Black Death. Years later though, many villeins were still unhappy because of new laws and taxes. This is the story of when the villeins, or peasants, rose in revolt against the lords and the Church.

It is 1381. The King's tax collector arrives in Brentwood in the South of England

I have come to collect the new tax. Each of you must pay.

The villeins were already annoyed. This was the last straw

Are you going to pay, John?

No chance!

These rebels throw the tax collector out of the town. Three of his helpers are killed

Get out and don't come back!

Soon villeins are rebelling all over the South East of England

Who do these villeins think they are?

The manor house makes a good bonfire!

20,000 villeins march towards London, led by Wat Tyler

What will we do when we get there?

Wat Tyler says we'll meet the King and ask him to put things right

As the villeins gather outside the walls of London the King comes to speak to them from a boat on the River Thames.

What do you want?

We will talk when you land my lord

Don't land my lord. It is too dangerous

Look! He's sailing back into the city

Why does'nt he land?

The King and his lords think they are safe behind the City walls, but inside...

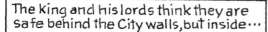

Quick, open the gate and let 'em in. Lords and bishops are no friends of ours

Once inside the villeins *riot*, smashing and burning the houses of the rich.

Break down the doors!

At the Tower of London they find the *Archbishop* of Canterbury.

Die, traitor!

Arghh!

The Lord Mayor of London acts to protect his city.

Loyal citizens of London, arm yourselves and meet me and the King at Smithfield on Saturday morning!

We must defend ourselves before we are all killed!

The two sides meet

Tyler! Tell me what you want!

I'll tell you alright!

But as Tyler moves forward the Lord Mayor stabs him to death

Arghh!

Without their leader, the villeins are lost

What do we do now John?

Dont ask me

I don't like the look of the Lord Mayor's lot

The King speaks to them

I will be your leader. Follow me from this city and you will come to no harm. Return in peace to your villages

Seems like a good idea to me John

The peasants go back to their homes. But soon.....

Quick John, hide! The king's soldiers are looking for the people who went to London!

Many villeins are hanged

String him up lads!

That will teach 'em a lesson

Villeins you were, and villeins you will stay!

WORKFILE

1 Copy the table below. It shows the main events of the Peasants' Revolt. But they are in the wrong order.

Work out the order in which the events happened. Fill in the middle column with numbers 1 to 6, putting 1 beside the first event, 2 by the second, and so on. The first two have been done for you.

2 Think about each of the events in the table below. What do they show us about the people who took part? Choose from the list opposite.

(Do the others in your group agree with you?)

Fill in column three of your table. Write the correct statement by each event.

- Many villeins hated religious leaders.
- The King did not expect to keep his promises.
- Some people in London were on the villeins' side.
- The villeins did not want to rule the kingdom themselves.

Event	Order (1–6)	Showed . . .
The gates of London were opened for the villeins to enter the city.	2	
The Archbishop of Canterbury was murdered.		
The villeins did not try to kill the King when they met him.		
Many manor houses were burnt as the villeins marched through Kent.	1	
After the villeins returned home the King ordered hangings to punish the leaders of the revolt.		
The Lord Mayor of London formed an armed band of men to help the King.		After the riots in London, many Londoners wanted to get rid of the villeins.

8 How Do We Know About the Past?

evidence, **monk**, **chronicle**, recorded, Latin, translated, **quill**

You have read the story of the Peasants' Revolt. Did the author make it all up like in a comic? The events of the Peasants' Revolt happened over 600 years ago. How do we know what really happened so long ago?

Evidence

One way we can try to find out about the past is to find some evidence. There is some 600-year old evidence left for us to look at about the Peasants' Revolt.

A monk at work

Some of this evidence was written by monks at the time the events happened. These writings were called chronicles.

Chronicles

Some monks spent many hours writing each day. They wrote in large books. They recorded important events which they had heard about.

This is part of a page from a chronicle. It is written in Latin. It has to be translated before we can understand it. We still have many chronicles. They are old books and are kept in special places in some churches and museums.

WORKFILE

1 Draw a labelled picture of a monk writing a chronicle. Show what he might be thinking. Use these labels:

quill   chronicle

2 Write a few sentences of a chronicle. Describe part of the Peasants' Revolt. Try to make your writing look like a real chronicle. You might even try to make and use a quill pen to write it with.

3 Think about some things which have happened in the world recently. How do you know what happened? What evidence have you seen or heard?

Make a list of at least four ways in which the news reached you (eg newspaper, TV).

(Have the others in your group chosen the same ones?)

4 Look at the table below. Match up the word in the first column with the sentence which best describes it. Copy the table in its new order.

Recorded	Medieval books written by monks.
Chronicles	Something which tells us what happened.
Evidence	Written down to help people remember.

History Jury

reliable, **beheaded**

Just like the jury in a court, sometimes we have to decide how much we believe a piece of evidence from the past. Is it reliable?

One way we can do this is to compare different pieces of evidence to see if they agree. Historians compare many pieces of evidence to try to find out what happened in the past.

Look at the two sources, one below and one on the next page. They tell of the murder of the Archbishop of Canterbury. In what ways do the sources agree? Do they disagree?

Source A

'A group of villeins moved to the Tower of London. They dragged out the Archbishop and the Treasurer onto Tower Hill and beheaded them there.'

From *The Westminster Chronicle*, 1381–1394.

Source B

The murder of the Archbishop of Canterbury

WORKFILE

1 Study Sources A and B carefully. Decide what each Source tells us. Copy the table opposite. Tick the correct column. Sometimes you will have to tick both columns.

2 a Write a sentence or two to show how the two sources agree.
b Write a sentence or two to show how the two sources disagree.
c Which source tells the truth? Write a sentence or two to say which source you believe the most and why.

(Do the others in your group agree with you?)

	Source A	Source B
Shows that three men were killed.		
Shows that they were killed by a mob.		
Shows that they were beheaded.		
Shows that the Archbishop was killed.		
Shows that they were killed with swords.		
Shows that the killers had no mercy.		
Shows that the victims were taken outside from the tower.		

9

The Holy Land

Muslim, Jew, Christian, pilgrim, atlas

Look at this map. It shows countries in a part of the world called the Middle East. The shaded part of the map shows an area known as the Holy Land.

There is a city called Jerusalem. It is an important holy city for people of three different religions: Muslims, Jews and Christians.

The Holy Land

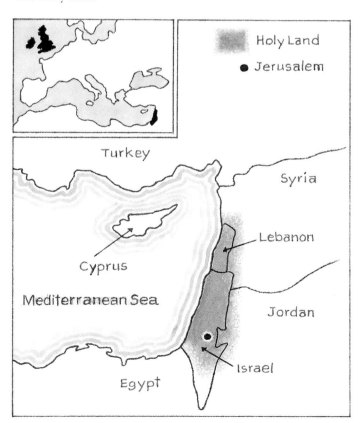

People from all over the world still visit Jerusalem. They hope to strengthen their religious faith. They are called pilgrims.

Medieval Pilgrims

There were many pilgrims to the Holy Land in medieval times. Christians went from England and France. Some went from Italy and Germany. All sorts of people. It was a long and dangerous journey by land and sea.

But 900 years ago there was trouble in the Holy Land. War broke out. Muslims and Christians fought each other. They both wanted to rule the Holy Land.

WORKFILE

1 Unscramble these words. Copy them down with their clues.

Clue	Word
Two religions	ulsimM
	nhitCrsia
Holy city	uJmeaserl
Religious travellers	gpmsilir
Middle East	yoHl aLdn

2 Make a list of the modern countries in the Middle East. (Get together in groups and look in an atlas or a newspaper.)

Crusader and Turk

Who Were the Turks?

Turk, Islam, invader, Allah, Crusader,
prophet, Jesus Christ, revenge

The Turks had ruled the Holy Land since 1076.
Their armies had marched into the Holy Land
looking for new land to settle in. They were
fierce warriors. They believed in fighting all the
enemies of Islam. (Islam is the Muslim religion.)

We must fight all the Christian *invaders* who do not believe in *Allah*, the one true God. These *Crusaders* do not follow the words of the great *prophet* Mohammed. They must never rule our Holy Land.

Who Were the Crusaders?

Many Christians from France, Italy, Germany and England formed armies. Most were experienced soldiers. They travelled to the Holy Land to fight. It was a long and slow journey. They were called the Crusaders.

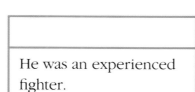

I must go to the Holy Land to fight the Turks. I believe that *Jesus Christ* is the Son of God. The Turks do not believe this. They murder our Christian pilgrims. They are not fit to rule the holy city of Jerusalem.

WORKFILE

Copy this table. Think about each of the statements. Do they fit in with what you know about the Crusader or the Turk?

Put a tick in the correct box. Some might fit both the Crusader and the Turk.

	Crusader	Turk
He was an experienced fighter.		
He believed there was one God called Allah.		
He believed it was right to fight for his religion.		
He believed he was defending his own land.		
He was fighting in a foreign land.		
He was fighting to gain revenge.		

10

Fighting Men

lance, crest, chain mail

Look carefully at this picture of a Crusader knight. It was drawn in medieval times.

Source A

WORKFILE

1 Look at Source A. Draw a picture of a Crusader knight. Put these labels on your picture:

sword, lance, family, crest, Crusader, cross, horse, chain mail

2 These sentences explain each of the labels on your drawing. See if you can match the labels with their sentences.

Write down the label and the sentence together.

- The sign of a Christian.
- Used for hand-to-hand fighting.
- Helped your friends to see where you were in battle.
- Used to kill enemies with when charging.
- Used to protect you from attack.
- Used to carry you into battle.

Then and Now

Look at this picture. It is a photograph of a modern soldier. Compare it with the picture of the Crusader knight opposite.

	soldier	Crusader
Can kill an enemy at long range.		
Can kill an enemy at short range.		
Has some form of transport.		
Can move easily in fighting gear.		
Needs to know a lot about weapons.		
Body protected by armour.		
Uses explosives.		
Well trained and experienced.		

similar, different, weapons, transport

In what ways are these two fighting men similar? In what ways are they different? Think about their clothing, weapons and transport.

(Do the others in your group agree with you?)

WORKFILE

Copy this table. Think about each statement. Do you think it best fits the soldier or the Crusader? Some of the statements fit both of them.

Do the others in your group agree with you?

Put a tick in the correct column(s).

Battles

battles, **bias, recruit**

There were many battles during the Crusades. Look at these pictures. They give you some idea of how a battle was fought.

Source A

Source B

Source C

Look at the sources carefully and then answer these questions in sentences.

1 What weapons can you see being used?

2 How have the soldiers tried to protect themselves? (Think of at least three ways.)

3 **a** What differences can you see between the Christian and Turk soldiers in Source A?
   b How is the man in the lower left corner of Source B being killed/injured?
   c How has the man at the bottom of Source C been killed?

(Do the others in your group agree with you?)

Bias

The pictures opposite show Turks and Crusaders fighting. They were drawn in medieval times.

Are they fair to both sides? Or did the artist want to make one side look better than the other? If the picture tries to show one side in a better light than the other it is 'biased'.

Look again at the pictures. Decide if the artist was biased by answering these questions. (Discuss them with the others in your group.)

● Can you work out which are the Turks and Crusaders? (Look for the Crusader cross.)
● Is one side winning?
● Do you think the artists were telling the truth with their pictures? Or did they favour one side more than the other?

WORKFILE

1 Write two or three sentences to say what you have decided.
2 Look again at the picture of a modern soldier below.

It was taken from an advert in a popular magazine. It is intended to attract recruits to the army.

Do you think the advert is biased? Think about the questions below to help you work it out. (Discuss them with the rest of your group.)

a How does the advert make the soldier look powerful? Do you think he would be difficult to beat in a battle?

b What does the advert tell you about 'enemy' soldiers?

c What sort of weapons do you think enemy soldiers would have?

d If people thought about enemy weapons do you think they would be more likely to want to join the army or less likely?

Is the advert biased?
Write two or three sentences to say what you have decided.

The Battle of Hattin, 1187

rank, din, **Saladin,** drew up, **Arab,** charge, fell upon, retreated, glee, **routed**

The battle of Hattin

'The Crusaders were like mountains on the march. Wave upon wave of them, their ranks crowded together. You could hardly see. The din almost knocked you out. The horses' hooves dug up the earth. The knights were weighed down by their armour and weapons. Ahead of them Saladin drew up his troops and decided to fight. All this was on a burning hot day.'

Written shortly after the battle by Ibn al Athir, an Arab historian.

Source B

'From the hilltop the Crusaders made a brave charge and drove the Muslims back. Then our men fell upon the enemy who retreated up the hill. I cried out with glee but they charged again and drove our men back. Again our men drove the enemy up the hill. I cried "we have routed them!"'

Written shortly after the battle by Al Afdal, son of Saladin.

WORKFILE

These sources tell you about one battle during the crusades.

1 Try to imagine what the battle would have been like. What sounds would you have heard?

Write a report of the battle as if you were one of the Crusaders in the picture. THINK . . . your story might be a bit different to the one you have read. Why? (clue . . . .BIAS).

Write about:

- Before the battle.
- The start of the battle.
- The fighting.
- The end of the battle.

Use these words to help you:

trample,   armour,   chain mail, bow and arrow,   charge,   sword,   chop, cut,   lance,   horse,   helmet.

12 Capturing Towns

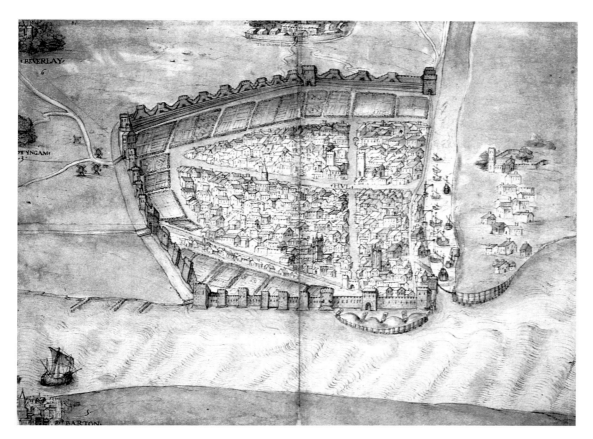

The Town of Hull in medieval times

capture, **siege**

Walled Towns

Look at this picture of a town. It was drawn in medieval times. The people of the town have made themselves safe by building a wall around the town.

WORKFILE

Study the picture. Then copy this paragraph and fill in the missing words. Choose from those in brackets.

The town had walls on three sides. The other side was protected by the _____ (sea, marsh, river). There were _____ (five, one, eight) holes in the walls so that people could pass in and out of the town. These were called gates. There were _____ (towers, slits) in the wall to fire arrows through.

Sieges

Many of the towns in the Holy Land were protected by walls. They were very difficult to capture. If the Crusaders or Turks wanted to capture a town they would start a 'siege.'

How to Besiege a Town

attack, **siege tower, sappers, molten, mangonel, trebuchet,** spies

Suppose you were the leader of a Crusader army. It is your job to capture the town of Al Bizar. The town is held by Turks and is protected by a strong wall.

Here are three methods you might try.

Attack

You might try to attack the town. In this picture several methods are being used.

A *siege tower* is placed alongside the town walls. Your men can then climb up and over the wall

molten lead

Skilled soldiers called *Sappers* dig into the wall. They fill the hole with wood and then set fire to it. This causes part of the wall to fall down

Trebuchet

Mangonel

The *mangonel* and the *trebuchet* are wooden machines used to throw large rocks. These rocks break down the walls and kill defenders

Spies

You might try to send spies into the town. They can tell you what is going on inside. They might be able to open a gate to let your army in.

Siege

You might surround the town and try to starve out the defenders. This might take a long time. For example in 1191 it took the Crusaders nine months to capture the town of Acre.

Siege Commander

Now you know how to capture a town, think about how your army is going to capture Al Bizar.

You arrived at Al Bizar yesterday. You have surrounded the town and the siege has started. Some of your soldiers have begun to put the siege machines together.

Study the picture below. It will tell you more about your army's position. (You have a few problems to think about.) Then read the next page.

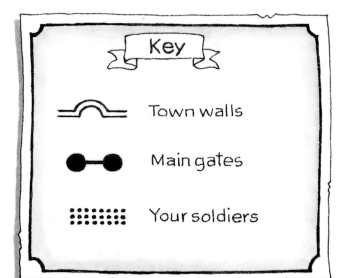

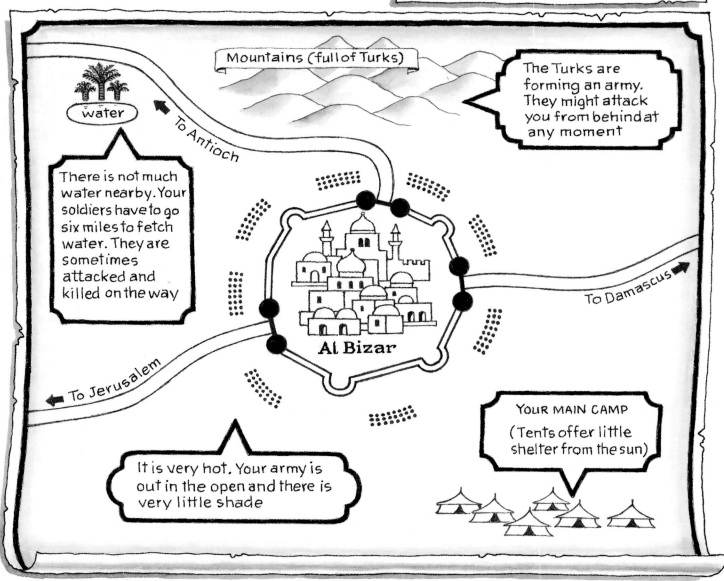

surrender, **tactic, morale**

You have to decide the best way to capture the town of Al Bizar. You have two choices. You can do one of the following:

- Attack the town as soon as your machines are ready (this will take three days).
- Wait for the town to surrender.

You should discuss tactics with the other commanders in your group.

Read the following items before you make up your mind. Think about each one carefully. Then make your decision.

Remember. If you get it wrong the whole crusade might fail!

Time
Your spies have reported to you. They think the town has about 20 days of water left.

Conditions
Once inside the town there will be shelter from the sun.

Morale
You have to keep up your soldiers' **morale**. Do you think they would rather fight or sit it out?

Losing men
About 500 men will be killed in the fighting if you attack.
But every day 50 soldiers will die of heat stroke when you are outside the town.

WORKFILE

Write a few sentences to say what you have decided and why.

You might mention:

- heat stroke
- water
- casualties
- morale

What were the views of the other commanders in your group?

13 *Castles*

A Crusader castle

retreat, defence, features, outer, inner

After they had captured parts of the Holy Land the Crusaders had to keep control. Many of the people who lived there were Muslims. They were not friendly. How could the Crusaders protect themselves in times of trouble?

WORKFILE

1 Look at the above photograph of a castle. It was built by a group of Crusaders. There were many Crusader castles built in the Holy Land. Crusader knights would retreat into them when there was trouble. The castles were built with defence in mind.

2 Copy this list of some of the features of the castle. Then look at the picture again. See if you can pick out the features on the list. Write the number by each one.

Feature	Number
Steep hill for outer defence.	
Round towers in outer wall.	
Steep rock sides to inner defence.	
Outer wall.	
High walls for inner defence.	
Round towers in inner walls.	

Design a Castle

Now see if you can design a castle of your own.

First look at the table below. It might give you some ideas.

On the left side are some more features of the castle in the last picture. Have another look.

On the right side you can see how each feature made the castle easier to defend.

Towers stick out of the walls	Defenders can shoot along the walls with bows and arrows
Round towers	No corners to be knocked off by flying stones
Very thick stone walls	Hard to break down with flying stones
Built on a mountain top	Attackers had to struggle uphill
Very high walls	Siege towers would not be high enough
Tall rock sides below the inner walls	Hard for sappers to dig holes in and under the walls
Deep well inside the castle	Plenty of water for many months

WORKFILE

OK. Now it's your turn.

Suppose you are a leader of a Crusader army. You want to build a castle to help you defend part of the Holy Land.

(You might discuss your plans with the other commanders in your group.)

Think about:

- Where you will put your castle.
- What it will be built of.
- What shape it will be.

1 Draw a picture or plan of your castle. Label its main features.

2 Write a sentence about each of these features.

14 What Happened When?

Saladin, Richard, timeline

The trouble in the Holy Land lasted a long time. Sometimes the Turks and Crusaders would be fighting. Sometimes they would live in peace for a while. Then fighting would break out again. A new Crusader army would set out from Europe. There were seven Crusades in all.

These two pages will help you sort out what happened when.

WORKFILE

The table below shows the main events of the first three Crusades. But the time periods are not in the right order. Each period should follow on from the last one. Look at the dates. Try to sort them out.

Copy the table but make sure you put the time periods in the right order. Your table should start with the period 1056–1096.

Colour each of the empty boxes in the first column with a different colour.

Colour	Time period	What happened	Winners Turks or Crusaders?
	1056–1096	Turks take control of the Holy Land.	Turks
	1144–1188	Turks have a new leader – Saladin. They re-capture Jerusalem and most of the Holy Land.	
	1097–1143	Crusaders take control of the Holy Land. They capture Jerusalem and build castles.	
	1192–1200	Saladin and Richard make peace.	
	1189–1191	New Crusade led by King Richard I of England wins some battles but does not re-capture Jerusalem.	

Crusades Timeline

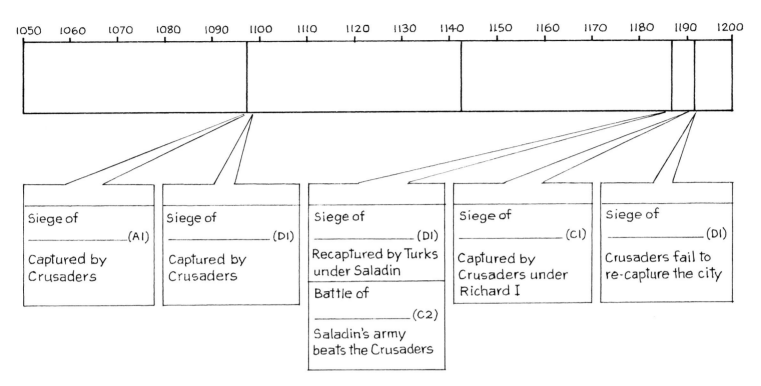

The timeline above tells you about some more Crusade events and when those events happened.

A1, C1, C2 and D1 refer to the squares on the map on the right.

1 Notice that the timeline has been divided up into the same time periods that you used in your table.

   a Copy the timeline and colour in the time periods using the same colours for each period that you used in your table.

   b Copy the writing in the boxes and use the clues (A1, C1, C2 and D1) to look up the places on the map. For example, Jerusalem is in the square D1. Write the place names in your timeline boxes.

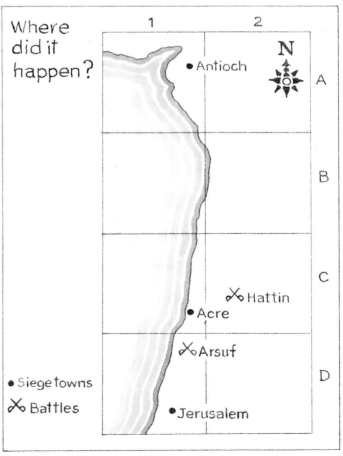

Glossary

Allah – Muslim name for God

Arab – Muslim from the Middle East

archbishop – head of the Church in England

baron – very important lord

beheaded – head chopped off

biased – one sided

chain mail – armour made from chains

Christian – religious follower of the teachings of Jesus Christ

chronicle – written record of events

crede – poem

crest – pattern or picture on armour etc to identify the person wearing it

Crusader – Christian fighter in the Holy Land

darn – mend holes in clothes

disease – illness

epidemic – disease spreading rapidly to many people

evidence – item(s) providing proof about something

furrow – narrow trench

hob – stone or metal plate where a fire is built

Islam – religion founded by prophet Muhammad

invader – person who takes over other people's land

Jesus Christ – religious leader believed by Christians to be the Son of God

Jew – follower of the Jewish religion

lance – long pointed pole used for fighting

mangonel – siege machine used to hurl stones

medieval – period of history

molten – melted

monk – person who lives in a community devoted to God

morale – mood

Muslim – follower of Islamic religion founded by the prophet Muhammad

oxen – plural form of 'ox' (an animal similar to a cow)

paving – stone floor

peasant – farmer owning little land

pilgrim – traveller on a religious journey to a holy place

plague – deadly type of disease

ploughing – digging soil over

prophet – person who some believe to be appointed by God to carry his message

quill – pen made from a feather

rank – lines of soldiers

rebel – revolt/fight against rulers

recruit – get people to join army etc

riot – violent gathering of people

routed – beat an army in battle so that their soldiers run away

Saladin – leader of the Muslim Turks

sapper – skilled miner and/or builder used to help an army break through walls of a besieged town or castle

siege – use force to surround a place and let no one in or out

siege tower – wooden tower used to attack castles or city walls

spinning – making thread

source – item(s) providing information about something

sowing – putting seeds in the ground

symptom – sign of disease on a patient

tactic – plan of attack

tax – money or goods paid to a king or government

tithes – goods given to the Church

traitor – person who breaks a trust put in him

trebuchet – siege machine used to hurl stones

trestle – separate wooden legs to hold up a table

Turk – person from central Asia

villein – farmer owning a small amount of land